A Comprehensive Guide to Planning for Your Adult Child with Disabilities

A Comprehensive Guide to Planning for Your Adult Child with Disabilities

Dayanand Shahapurkar

Copyright © 2023 by Dayanand Shahapurkar
All rights reserved.

ISBN 979-8-9888281-0-5

No portion of this book may be reproduced in any form without written permission from the publisher or author, except as permitted by U.S. copyright law.

This publication is designed to provide accurate and authoritative information in regard to the subject matter covered. It is sold with the understanding that neither the author nor the publisher is engaged in rendering legal, investment, accounting or other professional services. While the publisher and author have used their best efforts in preparing this book, they make no representations or warranties with respect to the accuracy or completeness of the contents of this book and specifically disclaim any implied warranties of merchantability or fitness for a particular purpose. No warranty may be created or extended by sales representatives or written sales materials. The advice and strategies contained herein may not be suitable for your situation. You should consult with a professional when appropriate. Neither the publisher nor the author shall be liable for any loss of profit or any other commercial damages, including but not limited to special, incidental, consequential, personal, or other damages.

Typesetting and cover design by Kent Mayne, kentmayne.com

Contents

I.	Introduction	1
II.	Understanding the Needs of Your Adult Child with Disabilities	7
III.	Legal Planning	23
IV.	Financial Planning	31
V.	Housing Options	37
VI.	Building a Support Network	45
VII.	Preparing Your Adult Child for Transition	53
VIII.	Encouraging Parents to Take Action	59
IX.	Looking Ahead	65
X.	Appendices	67
XI.	Acknowledgments	85

CHAPTER I

Introduction

Embarking on a journey of a thousand miles may seem daunting initially, but as the saying goes, it all begins with a single step. For parents and caregivers of young adults with disabilities, this journey is centered on one vital task – planning for their child's future. Why is this first step so crucial, you might ask? Well, the answer lies in the power of good planning. A well-thought-out plan can give our young adults confidence and care, leading to a content and thriving future. This process also helps them feel independent and confident about their future.

This book acts as a roadmap to guide parents and caregivers. The chapters give valuable information on recognizing your child's skills and teaching them life lessons. It explains how their learning journey at school can contribute to their success. This roadmap involves young adults promoting independence and self-assurance.

INTRODUCTION

Figure 1. A book as a roadmap for the parents and caregivers of adult children with disabilities.

But why start now, you may wonder? The sooner we plan, the more time we have to prepare for what lies ahead. It's much like setting off on a journey – you would want to leave packing at the last minute, would you? Early planning ensures everything is in place for the trip, making it a smoother, less stressful process.

To illustrate the significance of planning, we'll delve into the experiences of two families – the Smiths and the Johnsons. The story of the Smith family provides a glimpse into the positive impact of robust planning. The Johnson family's experience is a reminder of the risks of inadequate planning.

The highlight of this book is its simplicity. The language is easy to read and understand, intended to make everyone feel confident about planning for the future.

When discussing planning for the future, we often liken it to preparing for a grand adventure. For young adults with disabilities, this plan serves as their roadmap, guiding them toward their dreams. Like a detailed map, a well-crafted plan helps our young adults understand what they need to feel happy and perform at their best.

The best time to kick-start this planning process is right now. An early start to planning is akin to packing well for a trip. It ensures everything is ready and in its place, making the journey smoother and less frantic.

But what does this planning involve? At its core, it's about considering our young adults' unique needs and aspirations. The plan outlines the steps to help them realize these dreams. It might involve identifying an excellent school, acquiring vital skills, or combining both. Think of each element of planning as packing the right gear for an adventure.

Understanding the importance of planning is akin to having a reliable compass – it always points us in the right direction. We should start planning quickly and consider the factors involved. This compass gives parents and caregivers the tools to lead young adults to a brighter future.

Now let's look at what this book offers. It starts with an introduction that underlines why planning for the future is crucial. Here, we explain why we must be proactive as parents and caregivers. This first chapter is our starting point and the first step in understanding our journey.

Figure 2. Parents with an adult child with a disability looking for the journey ahead

Next, we step into the world of our kids. This chapter is like a key that opens the door to our child's universe. It sheds light on various aspects of their lives, such as their health, friendships, emotions, rights, and financial matters. By delving deep into each of these areas, we can gain a proper understanding of their needs.

Legal matters can often seem like a maze, challenging to navigate and understand. That's where our third chapter comes in. It simplifies legal jargon and explains essential terms such as 'guardianship' and 'conservatorship.' Consider this chapter as a friendly lawyer, decoding the complex legal language to protect our kids better.

INTRODUCTION

Chapter four brings us to financial planning. Here, we learn about handling money matters to ensure our child's financial security. We cover topics like special needs trusts and ABLE accounts, offering tools and plans to protect our child's financial future.

The fifth and sixth chapters discuss housing options and building a support network. Here, we explore different living options to envision a comfortable home for our kids. We also learn about creating a support network that cares about our child's well-being.

The seventh chapter focuses on preparing our kids for significant life transitions. This chapter guides us in teaching crucial life skills and crafting a comprehensive plan for these transitions.

The eighth chapter provides the motivation needed to take action. We share inspiring stories about successful families. It serves as a gentle nudge to act proactively and avoid potential pitfalls.

Finally, we offer a handy glossary, sample documents, checklists, and a frequently asked questions (FAQs) section. These resources are your go-to tools whenever you need to clarify a term, need a template, or have a question.

This book is easy to understand and simplifies the complex planning process for an adult child with disabilities. Through the power of storytelling and a tone of encouragement and support, we hope to inspire and reassure parents. You are strong, and your role is invaluable in shaping a promising future for your child. Your efforts, no matter how small they may seem, contribute significantly to a brighter future for your child. Every chapter read, every conversation held with another parent, and every step taken in this planning process brings us closer to that future.

So let this book be a reminder and a guide – you have the tools, the support, and the power to plan for a better future for your child. Each step you take is a step towards making that future a reality. And that's something truly commendable and worth being proud of.

This guidebook offers you a beacon of hope, a light that illuminates the path toward a brighter future for your child. Armed with this book, you are not alone in this journey. With every page, every chapter, we're right there with you, guiding you through each step of this vital process.

After the journey through the book, we reach the appendices, brimming with practical tools and resources. The appendices provide checklists, documents, and a glossary for your journey.

The FAQ section provides quick and easy reference information. Providing these resources empowers you with knowledge, making planning

INTRODUCTION

more straightforward and less overwhelming.

At the heart of this guidebook is the belief that parents and caregivers are the most potent force in shaping a young adult's future. You're not just the architects designing the roadmap but also the guiding lights illuminating the path. This book's stories, strategies, and resources strive to make planning more manageable and empowering.

The book is penned in a conversational style, using straightforward language that's easy to comprehend. We strive to engage parents and caregivers by making topics easier to understand and providing examples that are easy to relate to.

As you navigate this guidebook, we hope you feel more confident about planning for your child's future. Each chapter offers valuable insights, strategies, and examples.

This book will equip you with the tools needed to plan for your child's future. It encourages you to view every step as a significant milestone toward achieving your child's goal – a secure and fulfilling future.

Also, the book continues beyond providing resources and insights. It encourages an ongoing conversation and support network among parents and caregivers. By sharing your experiences, challenges, and victories, you can inspire and support each other, reinforcing the belief that you are not alone in this journey.

Planning your child's future may seem overwhelming, but you have the tools to make it easier. Your dedication, perseverance, and love for your child are your most potent allies in this journey. Remember, every step you take, no matter how small it may seem, is a step towards securing a better future for your child.

INTRODUCTION

Figure 3. A parent and their adult child with disabilities sitting together planning for future

This book is a comprehensive resource for your journey. Let the stories inspire you, the strategies empower you, and the resources guide you. With every page you turn, remember that you're one step closer to securing your child's bright and fulfilling future.

You have the resources and a community of support to begin this important journey. Remember, you're not alone in this journey; every step you take brings you closer to securing your child's bright and promising future. Let this book serve as a testament to your resilience, commitment, and undying love for your child. With every page you read, you're stepping towards crafting a better tomorrow for your child.

Together, we can turn the daunting task of planning for the future into an empowering journey of hope, resilience, and triumph. So, let's embark on this journey together, one step at a time, towards a future full of promise and potential for our children.

CHAPTER II

Understanding the Needs of Your Adult Child with Disabilities

As parents, understanding your child's needs can seem daunting. But guess what? You're already doing an incredible job just by engaging with this chapter. This journey can feel overwhelming but remember that you are not alone. We're here to help you understand more. We'll talk about five types of needs your child might have. These are medical, social, emotional, legal, and financial needs. Each one plays an essential role in your child's overall well-being.

Medical Needs

Caring for your adult child with disabilities involves attending to their unique medical needs. In this section, we will explore the various aspects of medical care and how you can ensure the well-being of your loved one. From ongoing medical care and therapy to managing emergencies and medications and utilizing adaptive equipment, each element plays a crucial role in their health and quality of life.

Ongoing Medical Care and Therapy involves regular medical care and therapy essential to keep your adult child with disabilities healthy and thriving. It is vital to schedule routine check-ups and appointments with healthcare professionals specializing in their needs. These visits serve multiple purposes, including monitoring overall health, identifying potential issues early on, and providing timely interventions.

Physical therapy focuses on improving your adult child's mobility, strength, and balance. Through tailored exercises and activities, a physical therapist can help them develop essential skills necessary for everyday tasks.

For example, Suppose someone you care about uses a wheelchair. In that case, physical therapy may involve exercises to strengthen their upper body, improve their range of motion, or enhance their ability to transfer independently. Additionally, physical therapy can address pain management and improve overall physical fitness.

Figure 4. A child with a disability engaged in physical therapy, guided by a therapist

Occupational therapy is designed to help individuals develop the skills required for daily living and enhance their independence. Occupational therapists work closely with your adult child to address specific challenges they may face in activities such as dressing, eating, grooming, and using assistive devices effectively. They focus on improving coordination, fine motor skills, cognitive abilities, and sensory processing to enable greater participation and engagement in meaningful activities. Occupational therapy also involves modifying the environment to enhance accessibility and safety.

Speech therapy is crucial for individuals who experience difficulties with communication or swallowing. A speech therapist can help your adult child improve their speech clarity, language skills, and overall communication abilities. They may use various techniques, exercises, and tools to enhance speech production, understanding, and social interaction. Speech therapy can also address challenges related to swallowing, ensuring safe and efficient eating and drinking.

While we hope for the best, preparing for unexpected medical emergencies and hospitalizations is essential. As a caregiver, you should have a plan to address such situations swiftly and effectively. This includes having a list of emergency contacts readily accessible, including primary healthcare providers, specialists, and hospitals. Being aware of the signs that warrant immediate medical attention is crucial. These signs may include severe pain, difficulty breathing, changes in consciousness, or any sudden and significant change in your adult child's condition.

Familiarize yourself with emergency protocols and procedures, such as CPR and first aid techniques. Additionally, ensure that relevant medical information, such as allergies, current medications, and existing medical conditions, is easily accessible. Keeping a record of this information in a centralized location, such as a medical information binder or an emergency app on your smartphone, can save valuable time in emergencies.

Managing medications is critical to caring for your adult child with disabilities. Ensuring they receive the prescribed medications at the proper dosages and times is essential. Develop a system to keep track of their medications, such as a pill organizer or digital reminders. The organization is critical, especially if multiple drugs are involved. Consider using color-coded pill organizers or electronic medication management systems that provide audible or visual alerts to help maintain consistency and accuracy.

Regular communication with healthcare providers is vital for monitoring the effectiveness of the medications and addressing any concerns or potential side effects. Keep an updated list of medications, allergies, and emergency contacts, and ensure that this information is easily accessible in case of medical appointments or emergencies. Be prepared to provide detailed information to healthcare professionals, including dosages, frequency, and any specific instructions or precautions related to the medications.

Adaptive equipment and assistive technology can significantly improve your adult child's independence and quality of life. These tools are designed to assist individuals with disabilities in performing daily tasks more effectively and comfortably. Examples of adaptive equipment include wheelchairs, walkers, canes, hearing aids, or specialized utensils. Assistive technology encompasses various devices, such as communication aids, voice recognition software, environmental controls, or intelligent home systems.

Working closely with healthcare professionals, therapists, and assistive technology specialists can help identify the most suitable adaptive equipment and assistive technology for your loved one's needs. They can assess their abilities, recommend appropriate devices, and provide training on how to use them effectively. Additionally, consider seeking funding options or assistance programs that can help cover the costs of adaptive equipment and assistive technology, as they can be significant investments.

Figure 5. A healthcare professional working with parents to identify the most suitable adaptive equipment and assistive technology for their child

By understanding and addressing your adult child's medical needs, you can help them lead a healthier and more fulfilling life. Regular medical care, therapy sessions, emergency preparedness, medication management, and adaptive equipment or assistive technology use all contribute to their overall well-being. Remember to consult with healthcare professionals, maintain open communication, and proactively seek support and resources. Your dedication and support as a caregiver are crucial in ensuring the best possible medical care and outcomes for your adult child with disabilities.

Social Needs

Understanding and addressing the social needs of your adult child with disabilities is essential for their overall well-being. This section will explore different aspects of socialization, support networks, and recreational activities that can enhance their social experiences and promote community integration.

Socialization and community integration are vital for individuals with disabilities to develop a sense of belonging and establish meaningful connections with others. Encouraging your adult child to participate in community events and activities can allow them to engage with others and be an active part of their community.

Look for community events that cater to your adult child's interests and abilities. Many communities organize inclusive events such as festivals, fairs, or cultural celebrations that welcome people of all abilities. Attending these events allows your adult child to connect with others, experience new things, and broaden their horizons. Encourage their participation and provide any necessary support to ensure they can fully engage in these activities.

Developing and maintaining friendships is essential for social well-being. Encourage your adult child to interact with peers and build meaningful relationships. This can be done through participation in social clubs, community groups, or volunteer activities. Please encourage them to join organizations or groups that align with their interests, whether a book club, a sports team, or an art class. These shared interests provide a common ground for connection and can lead to lasting friendships.

Support networks provide emotional support, guidance, and valuable information. They can help you and your adult child navigate the challenges and celebrate the successes of their journey.

Online support groups can provide a convenient platform for connecting with other caregivers and individuals with disabilities. These groups offer a space to share experiences, ask questions, and receive support from others who understand the unique challenges of caring for an adult child with disabilities. In-person support groups, on the other hand, provide an opportunity for face-to-face interaction and networking. Seek local support groups in your area that focus on disabilities or specific conditions to connect with others who share similar experiences.

Figure 6. A group of individuals with disabilities participating in a community event, showcasing socialization and community integration

Disability-specific organizations offer a wealth of resources and support for individuals with disabilities and their families. These organizations often provide advocacy, educational materials, workshops, and community events. They can connect you with others facing similar situations and give you a sense of belonging. Explore local and national disability-specific organizations relevant to your adult child's condition or disability to access valuable support networks and services.

Engaging in recreational activities and pursuing hobbies is essential for your adult child's overall well-being and personal growth. These activities provide enjoyment, skill development, self-expression, and socialization opportunities.

Special Olympics and adaptive sports programs offer inclusive sports opportunities for individuals with disabilities. These programs provide a supportive environment where your adult child can participate in various sports activities tailored to their abilities. They promote physical fitness, teamwork, and the joy of competition. Encourage your adult child to explore these programs and discover a sport they enjoy, whether swimming, basketball, track, field, or any other activity available in your community.

Art and music programs provide avenues for self-expression, creativity, and social interaction. Your adult child may find joy and fulfillment in exploring different art forms, such as painting, drawing, sculpture, or music. Look for local art classes, workshops, or music programs specifically designed for individuals with disabilities. These programs often offer adaptive techniques and accommodations to ensure everyone can participate fully. Engaging in artistic or musical activities can foster self-confidence, promote self-expression, and provide opportunities for showcasing talents.

By understanding and addressing your adult child's social needs, you can help them develop meaningful connections, establish a sense of belonging, and experience the joy of social interaction. Encourage their participation in community events, support their friendships and relationships, and utilize support networks and resources. Additionally, explore recreational activities and hobbies that align with their interests and abilities. You contribute to their overall happiness and fulfillment by nurturing their social well-being.

Emotional Needs

Understanding and addressing the emotional needs of your adult child with disabilities is crucial for their overall well-being and mental health. This section will explore different aspects of mental health support, stability, routine, and coping with change and loss.

Supporting your adult child's mental health is essential for their emotional well-being. By providing access to counseling and therapy and teaching coping strategies and stress management techniques, you can help them navigate their emotions and build resilience.

Counseling and therapy can provide a safe space for your adult child to express their thoughts and feelings, address any emotional challenges they may be facing, and develop strategies for coping. Seek out therapists who specialize in working with individuals with disabilities or have experience in the specific areas your loved one may need support. Regular sessions with a therapist can help your adult child process their emotions, improve their coping skills, and enhance their overall mental well-being.

Teaching your adult child coping strategies and stress management techniques equips them with valuable tools to navigate challenging situations. Please encourage them to explore techniques such as deep breathing exercises, mindfulness, journaling, engaging in hobbies they find relaxing or seeking sensory input through activities like listening to music or taking nature walks. Additionally, help them identify support systems, such as trusted friends or family members, whom they can turn to during stress. Empowering your adult child with effective coping mechanisms gives them a sense of control and resilience.

Establishing stability and routine is essential for promoting security and emotional well-being in individuals with disabilities. Consistency in daily schedules and maintaining familiar surroundings and caregivers can significantly contribute to their stability and happiness.

Create a structured daily schedule for your adult child, including regular routines for waking up, meals, activities, therapy sessions, and bedtime. Consistency provides a sense of predictability and can help reduce anxiety. Visual aids, such as visible schedules or calendars, can benefit individuals with disabilities as they represent the day's activities and help reinforce the daily routine. Involve your adult child in creating the schedule, giving them a sense of ownership and control over their daily activities.

Maintaining familiar surroundings and caregivers can improve your adult child's emotional well-being. Typical environments, such as their home or favorite places, provide comfort and security. Similarly, having consistent and reliable caregivers who understand their unique needs and preferences fosters a trusting and supportive relationship. Whenever possible, try to maintain stability in their living arrangements and ensure their caregivers are familiar with their routines, preferences, and any specific accommodations or support they may require. Encourage open communication between your adult child and their caregivers, enhancing their emotional well-being.

Change and loss can be particularly challenging for individuals with disabilities. It is essential to provide them with support and strategies to navigate these experiences, whether dealing with significant life transitions or losing a loved one.

If your adult child experiences the loss of a loved one or goes through significant changes, such as moving to a new home or transitioning to a different phase of life, consider seeking grief and loss counseling. Grief counselors can provide guidance, support, and coping strategies to help your adult child process their emotions, adjust to change, and navigate the grieving process. Encourage open and honest conversations about their feelings, validate their emotions, and provide a safe space for them to express their grief.

Effective planning is crucial when significant transitions are anticipated, such as moving to a new living arrangement or transitioning from school to post-school life. Collaborate with healthcare providers, educators, and support organizations to develop a comprehensive transition plan that addresses your adult child's needs, goals, and preferences. This plan should outline steps, supports, and resources to ensure a smooth transition and minimize potential emotional challenges. Involve your adult child in the planning process, encouraging their input and providing reassurance during times of change.

Addressing your adult child's emotional needs provides them with the tools, support, and stability necessary for their emotional well-being. Encourage access to mental health support, teach coping strategies, establish peace and routine, and provide guidance during change and loss. Understanding and nurturing their emotional needs can foster resilience, happiness, and a positive outlook on life.

Legal Requirements

Understanding and addressing the legal needs of your adult child with disabilities is essential to protect their rights, ensure their well-being, and provide them with the necessary support. This section will explore the importance of guardianship or conservatorship, understanding disability rights and advocacy, and how you can actively protect and advocate for your adult child's legal rights.

Figure 7. Parents of a child with disabilities in a courtroom discussing Guardianship

Guardianship or conservatorship is a legal process that grants an individual the authority to make decisions on behalf of another person who cannot make decisions independently. It is essential to clearly understand the roles, responsibilities, and considerations involved in this process.

Educate yourself about your jurisdiction's specific roles and responsibilities associated with guardianship or conservatorship. These responsibilities may include managing their healthcare needs, ensuring their financial well-being, and advocating for their best interests. It is essential to consult with legal professionals who specialize in disability law to gain a comprehensive understanding of your rights and obligations as a guardian or conservator.

If you consider becoming a guardian or conservator for your adult child, assessing your capabilities, availability, and commitment to fulfilling the responsibilities is crucial. Guardianship or conservatorship is a significant undertaking that requires careful consideration. Reflect on your ability to make decisions in the best interest of your adult child and provide the necessary care and support they need. Explore this option if you believe another family member, trusted friend, or professional may be better suited. Always prioritize your adult child's well-being and best interests when making this critical decision.

If someone else has been appointed as the guardian or conservator for your adult child, it is essential to maintain open communication and regularly monitor their actions. Stay informed about the decisions being made on behalf of your loved one and ensure they align with their best interests. Regularly communicate with the guardian or conservator, ask for updates, and express concerns or questions. It is essential to actively participate in your adult child's care and monitor the actions of the guardian or conservator to protect their rights and well-being.

Understanding disability rights and advocating for your adult child's rights are vital to ensuring their equal access, inclusion, and protection.

Please familiarize yourself with the Americans with Disabilities Act (ADA) and its provisions. The ADA prohibits discrimination against individuals with disabilities and mandates equal access to employment, public services, transportation, and accommodations. Understanding the rights afforded by the ADA can empower you to advocate for your adult child's rights and ensure they receive the necessary accommodations and support they are entitled to. Be aware of the specific provisions that apply to your adult child's disability and educate yourself on how to assert and protect their rights under the law.

Protect your adult child's legal rights by staying informed about relevant laws and regulations about their disability. Keep yourself updated on changes in legislation and advocacy efforts in your community. Join disability advocacy organizations or support groups that promote the rights of individuals with disabilities. These organizations often provide valuable resources, guidance, and opportunities to network with other advocates. Actively participate in advocacy campaigns, attend workshops or seminars, and utilize the available resources to ensure that your adult child's rights are upheld, and their voice is heard.

It is essential to recognize that each person's legal needs may vary, and consulting with legal professionals specializing in disability law can provide personalized guidance and support. By understanding and addressing the legal requirements of your adult child with disabilities, you can navigate the complexities of guardianship or conservatorship, protect their legal rights, and advocate for their inclusion and equal access. Seek legal advice when needed, stay informed about disability rights, and actively engage in advocacy efforts. Your dedicated efforts can ensure that your adult child's legal rights are upheld and their voice is heard.

By taking these steps, you can provide a solid legal foundation for your adult child with disabilities, ensuring their rights are protected and their best interests are represented.

Financial Requirements

Understanding and addressing the financial needs of your adult child with disabilities is essential for their long-term stability and well-being. This section will explore managing expenses and government benefits to ensure financial security.

Figure 8. Parent of a Child with Disabilities working with a Financial Advisor

Effectively managing expenses is crucial for your adult child's financial stability. Consider the following key areas when planning and budgeting:

Housing costs, including rent or mortgage payments, utilities, and maintenance fees, can be a significant part of the budget. Explore affordable housing options and consider government assistance programs that provide housing support for individuals with disabilities. Additionally, investigate potential modifications or accommodations needed in the living environment to ensure your adult child's safety and accessibility. Research home modification grants or low-interest loans that can help cover the costs.

Medical and therapy expenses are often ongoing for individuals with disabilities. Considering doctor visits, medication, assistive devices, and specialized therapy costs is essential. Review your health insurance coverage and understand the extent of the financial support it provides. Explore any available assistance programs, grants, or charitable organizations that offer financial aid for medical and therapy expenses. Additionally, research if your adult child qualifies for government healthcare programs or Medicaid waivers that can help offset these costs.

Daily living expenses, such as groceries, transportation, clothing, and personal care items, should be factored into the budget. Create a monthly spending plan that covers these essential needs. Consider ways to save money, such as utilizing coupons, buying in bulk, and exploring community resources that offer discounted or free services. Look into programs like the

Supplemental Nutrition Assistance Program (SNAP) that can provide additional assistance with food expenses.

Government benefits can provide crucial financial support for individuals with disabilities. Understand the available benefits and eligibility criteria to maximize your adult child's access to financial assistance.

Research and understand the government benefit programs available to your adult child, such as Supplemental Security Income (SSI) or Social Security Disability Insurance (SSDI). Familiarize yourself with the application process, required documentation, and deadlines. Seek assistance from social workers, disability advocates, or legal professionals who can guide you through the application process and help you compile the necessary information. Access the most up-to-date information and application forms through online resources and official government websites.

Figure 9. Parents of a Child with Disabilities in the Social Security Office

Each government benefit program has specific requirements and regulations. Educate yourself on the eligibility criteria, income limits, and reporting responsibilities associated with the benefits your adult child may be eligible for. Stay updated on any changes to the program requirements to ensure ongoing eligibility and compliance. Consider consulting with a benefits specialist who can provide personalized guidance based on your adult child's unique circumstances. They can help you understand the rules around income limits, resource limits, and how earnings may affect benefits eligibility.

Additionally, it is crucial to maintain organized records of your adult child's financial documentation, including benefit statements, medical bills, and receipts. This will help ensure accurate reporting and facilitate any necessary appeals or reviews of benefits decisions.

By effectively managing expenses and understanding government benefits, you can ensure the financial well-being of your adult child with disabilities. Plan and budget carefully, explore housing and medical assistance programs, and stay informed about available government benefits. Remember to review and update the financial plan as circumstances change regularly. Taking proactive steps and seeking expert advice can provide stability and economic security for your adult child's future.

Note: Financial planning can be complex and vary depending on individual circumstances. It is recommended to consult with financial advisors, disability advocates, or legal professionals with expertise in disability-related financial matters for personalized guidance.

CHAPTER III

Legal Planning

Welcome to Chapter 3, which is all about Legal Planning! What does that mean? Legal planning is like making a map for your adult child's future. It's about figuring out who will help them make big decisions or care for them when they can't.

We'll learn about big words like guardianship and conservatorship. These are fancy terms for people who help someone choose where to live, what doctor to see, or how to handle money. We'll also talk about the power of attorney when you pick someone you trust to make big decisions if you can't.

And we must remember the letter of intent! This isn't a law thing, but it's a scathing letter where you write everything someone needs to know to take good care of your adult child.

Sounds like a lot, right? Don't worry. We're going to make it easy to understand. By the end of this chapter, you'll feel ready to make an excellent plan for your adult child's future.

Guardianship and Conservatorship

Guardianship and conservatorship might sound like tricky words, but they're just fancy names for jobs some people do. A guardian is a helper who makes important decisions for someone who can't do it themselves. They could decide where this person lives or what doctor they go to. Imagine them like a team captain, ensuring everyone is where they need to be and doing what they need to do.

Figure 10. Parents in a Lawyer's Office Discussing Guardianship and Conservatorship

On the flip side, a conservator is like a piggy bank guard. Their job is to handle money stuff. The conservator must pay bills on time and make wise financial decisions. So, while a guardian takes care of the person, a conservator takes care of the person's money.

Both these jobs, being a guardian or a conservator, continue until they're no longer needed or until a judge, like a referee, decides it's time for a change.

Now, how does someone get one of these essential jobs? Well, it's like getting picked for a school team. First, they must meet with a judge, like meeting with a coach or a gym teacher. The judge will assess the situation and decide if a guardian or conservator is necessary.

Just like you wouldn't want anyone to be your team captain, you must be careful about whom you pick as a guardian or conservator. You want someone trustworthy, like your best friend. They should know your adult child's needs, like their favorite book. They should always be ready to speak up for their child like a friend would stick up for them.

In this section, we will learn more about being a guardian or a conservator. We'll find out what paperwork you need and discuss how to pick the best person for the job. It might seem scary but don't worry, we're in this together, and by the end, you'll be a pro!

Becoming a guardian or conservator isn't as simple as just saying you want to be one. Apply for it, like applying for student council at school. Don't just tell your friends you want to do it; let the principal know, too.

Here, the 'principal' is a judge. They need to know why your adult child needs a guardian or conservator. To show them why, provide some important papers. This might include a note from a doctor explaining your child's health or bank statements to show the money that needs to be taken care of. It's like when you're sick and need to give your teacher a note from your parents.

Finally, we must consider what makes a suitable guardian or conservator. We don't just pick our best friends to be on our team. We want the best players. Similarly, you want to choose someone reliable to make the best decisions for your child.

They must understand your child's needs, just like a teacher understands what each student needs to learn best. And they need to be ready to speak up for their child, like a big brother or sister standing up for their sibling.

So there you have it! That's what guardianship and conservatorship are all about. Remember, this may seem a lot now, but we will understand it all step by step. By the end of this, you'll know how to pick the best person to help your adult child and have a plan to make it happen.

Choosing the right person to be a guardian or conservator is a big deal. It's like picking the captain of your team. You wouldn't just like anyone, right? You'd want to choose someone reliable and who knows the game well. Pick someone trustworthy to be your guardian or conservator.

This person needs to understand your adult child's needs, like how an excellent teacher knows how each of their students learns best. Maybe your child needs help with certain things or likes doing things in a certain way. The guardian or conservator should know these things and consider them when deciding.

But here's something significant: just like a team captain needs to stand up for their team, a guardian or conservator needs to speak up for your child. They must ensure that your child's needs are met and treated fairly. This is called advocating, and it's a big part of their job.

By now, you've learned quite a lot! We know what a guardian and a conservator do, how to become one, and what kind of person would suit these roles. Keep going, and soon you'll know everything you need to make a solid plan for your adult child's future. Good job, and let's keep learning!

Power of Attorney

Let's move on to the next part of our journey – the power of attorney. The term sounds cool. It's just as important as it sounds. Think of it like a superhero power you give to someone you trust, so they can make critical decisions if you can't do it yourself.

There are two main types of powers that you can give someone. One is called a financial power of attorney. This person is like a trusted club treasurer who manages the money matters. They ensure they pay the bills on time and spend the money in the right places.

Figure 11. A Lawyer Discussing Power of Attorney Document with Parents

The other one is the medical power of attorney. This person is like a trusted team medic who makes health decisions if you can't. They can decide which doctor you should see or what treatment you should get.

So, how do you give someone this superhero power? First, you must choose someone you trust, like a friend who always keeps their promises. Then, you chat with them and let them know your wishes and what you expect them to do if they need to use their power.

Now, onto the letter of intent. Despite the formal name, it's a letter where you write down all the essential things about your adult child. It's like a handbook about your child for anyone needing to take care of them in the future.

You would include personal information, like your child's full name, date of birth, and medical history. You'd also write down their likes and dislikes, their routines, and who their essential friends are.

And just like how the world keeps changing, this letter should also be updated as things change. It's also a good idea to share copies of the letter with anyone needing it.

So, that's much information, but you're doing a great job following along! In the following sections, we'll go into more detail about the power of attorney and letters of intent and how they can help plan for your adult child's future. Keep going; you're doing fantastic!

Remember, a power of attorney is a superhero power you can give to someone else. They can use it to make crucial decisions on your behalf if you can't do it yourself.

Imagine if you had a superpower that you could share. You'd want to be careful who you gave it to, right? You'd pick someone who you know would use it wisely. That's what you must do when choosing an agent for your power of attorney. You want to pick someone as trustworthy as a superhero side-kick. This person should be someone who sticks to their promises and can make good choices, even when things are tough.

Once you've picked your 'superhero sidekick,' having a heart-to-heart talk with them is essential. You should tell them about your wishes and what you expect them to do if they need to use their power. For example, you could talk about what you'd want to happen if you were sick and couldn't decide about your treatment. Or you could discuss how you'd like your money to be managed if you need help.

Letter of Intent

A letter of intent is a chock-full of helpful information about your adult child. It's like a guidebook or manual that helps others understand your child's needs and wants. It's beneficial, like a treasure map leading to the best care for your child.

Start the letter of intent with basic information, like the opening chapter of a book. This includes your child's full name, date of birth, and other similar details. You might think everyone already knows this, but starting with the basics is always good.

Next, consider including their medical history, as a history book tells us about the past. This can help doctors or caregivers understand your child's health better. It's as if you had a puzzle, and each piece of medical history is a piece of the puzzle. The more details you have, the more complete the picture.

You'll also want to include details about your child's likes and dislikes. This is like sharing the secret recipe for their happiness. Do they enjoy long walks in the park or prefer playing video games? Do they like listening to music or reading books? This section should paint a clear picture of their personality and preferences.

Figure 12. Parents are working on the Letter of Intent Document

Remember daily routines. Our routines, like waking up at a particular time or eating certain foods, make us feel secure and comfortable. By sharing your child's habits, you're providing a blueprint for a smooth day. Someone can detail this as you'd like, from what they eat for breakfast to their bedtime ritual.

But wait, there's more! Also, include information about relationships in your child's life. Other people who play unique roles are present in your child's life, like different characters in a storybook. Teachers, friends, family members – include everyone who plays a crucial role in their life.

And just like a storybook gets new chapters, we should update this letter as your child's life evolves. You should review it often, updating details as necessary. This could be once a year or more often if a lot changes. It's like giving the guidebook new editions now and then.

Finally, share this important document with anyone who needs to know your child well. This could be family members, teachers, doctors, or future caregivers. It's like giving them a golden ticket to understanding your child better.

So, there you have it! That's what a letter of intent is all about. Remember, this isn't just a piece of paper. It's a lovingly created guide that helps ensure the best possible care for your child. It's a testament to your love and commitment to their well-being. So, take your time, and remember to update and share it regularly!

CHAPTER IV

Financial Planning

Now, we discuss planning your money if you or a loved one have unique needs. This part of the book is essential because it helps you learn how to make sure you have enough money for the future and how to use it best.

First, we'll talk about Special Needs Trusts. These are like safe boxes where you can keep money or other things of value. The best part is that this safe box does not affect getting help from the government.

Then, we'll learn about ABLE accounts. They are special bank accounts for people with disabilities. These accounts help save money without paying too much tax. Plus, we'll talk about who can have an ABLE account and how to use the money in it.

We will also talk about life insurance. It's a promise from a company to give money if something happens to the person insured. We'll see how to choose the best life insurance and who should get the money if something happens.

Lastly, we'll learn about help from the government, like SSDI, SSI, Medicaid, and Medicare. These programs can give money and health care to people who need them. We'll talk about who can get these benefits and how.

This chapter will ensure you know the best way to plan for the future if you or a loved one have unique needs.

Special Needs Trusts

This is a fantastic tool called Special Needs Trusts. Picture it like a treasure chest. You can store money and other valuable things in it, and the best part is that this is designed for the benefit of the person with special needs. Pretty cool, right?

FINANCIAL PLANNING

Figure 13. Parents in a Bank Manager's Office to Open Special Needs Trust

Now, there are three types of these treasure chests, or as we call them formally, Special Needs Trusts. Let's imagine you're a person with special needs and have your own money you want to protect. You can put this money into a First-party Special Needs Trust. Using a First-party Special Needs Trust ensures your money is secure and available.

But what if you're not a person with special needs and want to keep some of your money or property for a loved one with special needs? Well, the Third-party Special Needs Trust is like a gift box. Parents, relatives, or friends can put their money or property into this trust as a gift for their loved ones with special needs.

The last kind is slightly different but still a treasure chest. It's called a Pooled Special Needs Trust. Please consider this a community treasure chest where many people put their money. This big treasure chest is cared for by a group working for a nonprofit organization. Even though many people's money goes into the same chest, everyone's share is tracked separately, so you always know what you put in.

Special Needs Trusts are constructive. Do you know how superheroes protect people? These trusts protect the valuable assets of the person with special needs. And another superpower of these trusts is that they can help a person with special needs keep getting help from the government, like Medicaid. You might be wondering, how can a trust do that? The secret is that the money and property in the trust should be counted when the government decides if someone can get help.

But just like any superhero, there's always something to watch out for. Special Needs Trusts need a person to look after them, like a superhero sidekick. This person is called a trustee. The trustee makes sure the trust is being used properly. But sometimes, they need to get paid for their work, called fees.

So, what if you think a Special Needs Trust could be a superhero for you or your loved one? What do you do next? Find another kind of superhero-a lawyer who knows about special needs. This lawyer can guide you in putting money into the trust and choosing the right trustee. They can ensure they did everything correctly, and you benefit most from the trust.

Remember, like every superhero story, every Special Needs Trust is unique. It is essential to find the right trust that fits your account, ensure it's set up correctly, and choose the right trustee. With a Special Needs Trust, you can secure a happy ending for your financial story.

Life Insurance

Now, let's explore the world of Life Insurance, another incredible tool in our financial toolkit. Imagine life insurance as a superhero shield. It's something you set up now to protect your loved ones in the future. When you're no longer around, the 'shield' of life insurance protects your loved ones and ensures their financial security.

There are two main types of life insurance: 'shields.' The first is called Term Life Insurance. Think of this as a shield that's only around for a certain amount of time say 20 or 30 years. If something happens to you during that time, the protection springs into action and provides money, known as a death benefit, to your loved ones.

The other kind is Whole Life Insurance. This is like a shield that lasts your entire life. If you keep paying the insurance premium, which is like a monthly fee, this shield will be there. When the time comes, it provides a death benefit, just like term life insurance. But it also has a cool cash value feature, a savings account that grows over time.

FINANCIAL PLANNING

Figure 14. Parents Meeting with Insurance Agents to Discuss Their Needs

When you set up your life insurance, you can choose who gets the money from the shield if something happens to you. This person is called a beneficiary. You might wonder, "Can I name the Special Needs Trust as a beneficiary?" The answer is absolute! That way, the money goes into the trust and can be used for the person with special needs without messing up their government benefits.

But, like with all superhero tools, there are some things to watch out for. One is taxes. Usually, the money from life insurance is tax-free. But if you name the trust the beneficiary, I might owe some tax. It isn't straightforward, and talking to a financial superhero, like an accountant or lawyer, is a good idea to understand how it works.

Life insurance can be a powerful tool. It's not just for the rich or the old, but for anyone who wants to protect their loved ones. Weigh the pros and cons of term life and whole life insurance policies. It's your way of being a financial superhero!

So now you might think, "How do I choose between term life insurance and whole life insurance? Which one is the best shield for me?" Well, it's like choosing between different superheroes. They all have strengths, but the best depends on your needs and circumstances.

Let's look at term life insurance first. Term life insurance might be the right choice if you require insurance for a particular duration, such as until your kids are grown, or your home is paid off. The premiums (or monthly payments) for term life insurance are usually lower, so it's more affordable upfront. But remember, it only lasts for a specific term (like 10, 20, or 30 years), and it doesn't have that cash value feature we discussed.

Whole life insurance lasts your entire life! It's there for as long as you keep paying the premiums. The premium is higher because it includes that cool cash value feature (the part that acts a bit like a savings account). But it could be a good choice if you want to leave a guaranteed amount to your loved ones, regardless of when you pass away.

In life insurance, naming your beneficiary is like choosing your super-hero sidekick. If you have a special needs trust, you can call it your beneficiary to ensure they care your loved one for. This can be a smart move because it helps keep money in the trust and can prevent any issues with eligibility for government benefits.

But, like any superhero adventure, it can get a bit complicated. For example, there may be tax implications to consider. Life insurance payouts are usually tax-free, but some taxes might be involved if the money goes into a special needs trust. This is a time to call in a financial advisor or attorney, your Alfred, to help navigate the complex world of taxes.

Remember, choosing life insurance is a big decision, and there's no one-size-fits-all answer. Each person's situation is unique. So, think about your needs, talk to professionals, and make the right choice. It's your financial future, so you're the superhero in this story!

Government Benefits

Four pathways of government benefits are visible: SSDI, SSI, Medicaid, and Medicare. Each path has its unique characteristics and requirements, but they all share a common goal: to support and relieve individuals in need.

Let's start our exploration with Social Security Disability Insurance, com-monly known as SSDI. Think of SSDI as a 'piggy bank' you've contributed to during your working years, with part of your paycheck going towards Social Security. If a disability stops you from working, SSDI acts as a financial super-hero, releasing funds based on the amount you've contributed. Remember, the more you've put into your 'piggy bank' over the years, the higher your SSDI benefits will be. Solving the SSDI benefits puzzle can be difficult, but resources and professionals can help.

Next, we turn to Supplemental Security Income or SSI. Unlike SSDI, SSI isn't tied to your work history but is based on your financial needs.

Picture SSI as a superhero that swoops in when you're in a tight financial spot, providing the help you need to cover basic living costs. SSI is there for those who have yet to work much, or at all, and have few resources. The program provides a safety net to those most in need.

Now, let's journey to Medicaid, a program designed to help cover health-care costs for individuals with limited income. Medicaid provides essential healthcare services, like doctor visits and hospital stays. Medicaid is a life-line, ensuring that lower-income people can access necessary medical care.

Last, we come to Medicare, a program that primarily helps people aged 65 and over and some younger people with disabilities. Medicare is like a team of superheroes with unique abilities to cover various health-care needs. It's a comprehensive support system to help you manage your healthcare needs.

Navigating the world of government benefits can sometimes feel like a journey through a labyrinth, with twists, turns, and dead ends. But don't worry; you're not alone. Benefits counselors, social workers, and disability law attorneys can guide you. They can help you with eligibility, benefits, and the application process.

Remember, while SSDI, SSI, Medicaid, and Medicare each have their own set of rules and eligibility requirements, they all exist to help. They're like your personal team of superheroes, ready to lend their superpowers when you need them most. So don't hesitate to reach out for help when you need it. After all, even the greatest superheroes sometimes need a helping hand!

CHAPTER V

Housing Options

All right, let's journey into the world of housing options. This is a massive part of growing up, especially for people with special needs. Picking a place to live is more than just where you sleep at night. It's also about finding a spot to be happy, comfortable, and safe.

There are lots of different places where people with special needs can live. One option is group homes or adult foster care. This is like a big family home where people live together. They help each other and do fun things together, just like a real family. But remember, every family is unique. That means every group home is different, too. Some have more rules, while others let you do more things independently. Picking the right home is like picking out your favorite pair of shoes. They need to fit right and make you feel good.

Another option is called supported living arrangements. This is when you have your place, like an apartment or a house. But you also have helpers who come in to give you a hand with things you need. This can be stuff like getting dressed, finding a job, or even catching the bus.

There's also the choice of living with a family caregiver. This means staying with family who help take care of you. But just like when playing a team game, talking about who does what is super important. This helps everyone understand their job. Being a caregiver is a significant role, like being the team captain. So, it's essential to learn how to do it right and have friends and helpers to support you.

Deciding where to live is a big decision. So, it's okay to take time to explore all the choices. Like any adventure, finding the perfect home makes everything much more accessible. Now, let's get started and explore all our excellent housing options!

Adult Foster Care/Group Home

Let's dive deeper into the first housing option: adult foster care and group homes. Imagine being part of a big family living in a comfortable, welcoming house. That's what it's like in adult foster care or a group home. Picture it: a bunch of unique folks living together under one roof. The cool thing is that everyone gets help from caring for adults, such as meals, chores, and self-care.

Now, just like there are different pets, from goldfish to giant dogs, there are other types of group homes. Some are like cuddly kittens: they give you lots of attention and always help you. These homes have staff who are always there to help with everything, from waking up and getting ready for the day to preparing for bed. These homes are great for people who need more help with daily stuff.

Other group homes are more like birds: they allow you to spread your wings while keeping a safe nest ready. These homes let you do more independently, like choosing clothes, making the bed, or cooking meals. They're always there to lend a hand, but they also encourage you to do things independently. These are perfect for people who can do a lot alone but might need help now and then.

Figure 15. A Special Needs Boy In a Foster Care Home with a Caretaker

So, how do you pick the right home? Well, it's like choosing a new adventure book. You should check the cover, read the summary at the back, and flip through a few pages. That's what you do when picking a group home. You might visit some homes to see what they look like and how they feel. You get to ask questions too. What does the day look like in this home? What kinds of food do they cook? What fun things can you do there?

You'll also want to know about the people who work there. Think about them as the main characters in your adventure book. Are they kind, understanding, and patient? Do they know a lot about helping people with special needs? Do they stay in their jobs for a long time? And just as important, do they seem happy in their careers? You'll also want to meet your potential housemates. Do you think you'd get along? Do they seem like people you'd like to live with?

Choosing a group home is a big decision, like choosing your team in a game. You want to pick a place where you will be happy and feel safe. So, take your time, ask all the questions you want, and choose the home that feels right for you. Remember, it's not a race; it's about finding the right fit for you. So take a deep breath and enjoy the journey!

Supported Living Arrangements

Now, let's step into the world of supported living arrangements. This is another excellent housing option, and it's like having your castle but with a team of helpers whenever you need them. It's all about balancing being independent and getting the help you need.

In supported living, you can live in different places. You could rent an apartment in an extensive building like a mini castle. Or you could even own your own home, like having a big court all to yourself. Now, you might think that living alone sounds lonely. But here's the cool part: you can also share your home with others. This could mean having roommates, like in a group home, or even co-housing. Co-housing is when a group lives together in a community. Everyone has a home but shared gardens, playgrounds, or dining halls. It's like living in a village with your friends!

Now, even though you're living independently, you're not alone. Remember those helpers we talked about? They're here to help you with things like personal care. This could help with bathing, getting dressed, or brushing your teeth. Or they might help you with chores around the house, like cleaning or cooking. And don't worry if you need a hand with things outside the home, like going shopping or getting to a doctor's appointment; they can help with that too.

HOUSING OPTIONS

Figure 16 A Child with Disabilities in a Group Home with a Caretaker

But what if you want to work? Well, your helpers can support you with that too! They can help you find a job and learn how to do it well. They could help you write a resume, practice for a job interview, or learn new skills. Think of them like a coach in a sports team, guiding you and helping you do your best.

And guess what? If you need help getting around in your community, your team of helpers has got you covered. They can help you learn how to use public transportation, like buses or trains. Or they can teach you how to walk safely in your neighborhood. You won't have to miss out on fun activities in your community, like going to the movies or the park, because your team can help you get there and back.

The neat thing about supported living is that you customize your support. It's like ordering a pizza – you get to pick the toppings you want and leave off the ones you don't. You might need much help with some things and only a little with others, and that's okay. The goal is to help you live how you want, with the support you need.

Choosing a supported living arrangement is a big step towards independence. But remember, you're not alone in this journey. You have a team of helpers ready to assist you, and you can make choices about your life. So take your time, ask many questions, and make the right choice!

Family Caregiver

Think of your family as a unique team; your adult child with special needs is the most critical player. As their parent, you're like the coach, always thinking about the best way to support your child. One big decision is choosing a family member to be your caregiver.

Just like a coach has to pick the right player for a match, you must ensure this person is ready and able for this role. It's an enormous responsibility, like being chosen to play in a crucial game. So, ask: "Can they dedicate enough time each day to your child's care? Are they patient? Do they have the energy needed?" These are essential questions, just like a coach would need to know if a player is fit and has enough practice before a game.

HOUSING OPTIONS

Figure 17. A Child with a Family Caretaker

Being a caregiver can sometimes feel like learning a new sport. There will be new skills to learn, like dribbling a basketball or mastering the perfect swing in baseball. For instance, they might need to know how to administer medication, react in emergencies, or assist your child with daily activities like eating, bathing, or getting dressed.

Just as you wouldn't play a game of football on an uneven field, you also need to ensure your home is ready for this change. Are there ramps in the house if your child uses a wheelchair? If your child needs peace, is your house calm and peaceful? Like a well-prepared sports field, a safe, comfortable home is crucial.

A game plan is also vital. As the coach, it's up to you to decide who will do what and when. The family caregiver could help your child prepare for the day each morning, and you could step in to help with meals in the evening. This detailed plan helps everyone understand their roles and can prevent misunderstandings or problems before they even happen.

But remember, one player is only as strong as their support team. Like a critical player, a caregiver also needs a group for support. Please encourage them to find and connect with other people who are caregivers. This provides a platform to share experiences, gain valuable advice, and feel understood.

Regular check-ins with your child and the caregiver are vital, just like regular team huddles in a game. This ensures you know how they're feeling and if they're comfortable with the current arrangement. If something isn't working, you can change the plan, like a coach changes tactics during a game.

Choosing a family caregiver is a significant decision, akin to picking your star player for a championship game. But with love, careful planning, and a strong team, it could be the best choice for your child and your family. As winning a game takes teamwork, patience, and practice, so does this. Everyone can win in this game of life with the right strategy and game spirit!

CHAPTER VI

Building a Support Network

Building a support network is like making a team. When you're helping an adult child with disabilities, you need a good team. This team can help you with practical things and can be there to cheer you up when things get tough.

Let's think about your team as a big, warm group hug. Who's in the hug? Family and friends, experts who know much about disabilities, and people and places in your community. They all have a particular part to play in helping you and your adult child.

To build your team, start with the people closest to you, like your family and friends. It's important to talk to them about your hopes and plans for your adult child. Let them know how they can help. You might have a cousin who's excellent at paperwork or a friend who's a whiz at explaining things clearly. And it's always good to have a backup plan for when things don't go as expected.

Next up on your team are the experts. These are people like social workers, disability advocates, and doctors. Social workers can help you understand all the services and help you can get. Disability advocates are like superheroes for your adult child. They ensure your child is treated fairly and help with important legal matters. Disability advocates and social workers do this. Doctors and other medical professionals can help manage your child's health and make the right healthy choices.

Lastly, think about your local community. Some places in your neighborhood can be part of your team. Places like community centers and special clubs for people with disabilities. They can offer fun activities and programs where your adult child can meet others and make friends. Some places can help your child learn new skills and find work, which can be great for their confidence.

Figure 18. Local Community Event

So, that's your team – a mix of family, friends, experts, and community resources to support you and your adult child. You don't have to do this all on your own. With a strong team, you can face any challenge that comes your way.

Involving Family and Friends

First, it's all about talking and sharing. When taking care of an adult with disabilities, it is essential to share your plans with your family and friends, just like when playing soccer. All team members must know the strategy.

Talk to them about what you hope to achieve. Maybe your goal is to help your adult child learn a new skill or to join a community club. Share these plans with your family and friends. They might have some helpful suggestions or know someone who can help. It might be scary to share your fears, but remember, these people care about you and want to help. Sharing your worries can lighten your load and help others better understand how they can support you.

Now, it's about more than what you are talking about. It's also about listening. Ask your family and friends for their ideas. They might have some great thoughts that you hadn't considered. Your sister may know of a successful therapy; your best friend can suggest a local art club. Inviting their input makes them feel valued and a natural part of your support team.

Figure 19 Family Event

Another crucial part of involving family and friends is sharing responsibilities. Think about it like a school project. If you try to do all the work yourself, you'll get tired, and you might not do your best work. But if everyone does a small part, the project gets done well, and no one gets too tired.

It's the same with caring for an adult child with disabilities. Identify the areas where others can help. Your neighbor might be great at cooking and would be OK with preparing some meals for you. Your cousin might be a tech wizard and could help set up some helpful apps on your adult child's tablet. Be bold and ask for help; everyone can do something, no matter how small it seems.

Lastly, remember to create a backup plan. This plan is like your safety net. Do you know when you're playing a video game and have an extra life? Well, your backup plan is your different life. It's what you'll use when things don't go as expected. Your backup plan is to have a family member who can care for your adult child if you're unavailable. Or it's knowing that your friend can pick up your other kids from school if you have an emergency.

Building your support network with your family and friends is like building a team. Everyone has a part to play, and you can achieve much more together. So, keep talking, keep sharing, and remember, you're not in this alone. Your team is right there with you, ready to support you every step of the way.

Professional Support

Imagine you're on a team, a critical team. Your job is taking care of your grown-up child who has disabilities. Sometimes, this job might seem harsh. But guess what? You're not the only one on this team. Other professionals are eager to help.

Let's start with social workers. You can think of them as expert tour guides. When looking for services and resources to help your child, it can feel like you need help in a vast, confusing city. But the social workers know the city like the back of their hand. They can help you find local programs or even tell you about government help you might need to learn about. They're experts in finding the right paths in this city.

But the social workers' job continues. They also help during tough times, like a significant change or something terrible happens. It's like when a thunderstorm comes up during your city tour. The social workers have an enormous umbrella ready to help you get through the storm safely.

Figure 20. Parents of children with disabilities working with a social worker

Next on the team are disability advocates. They're like superheroes who fight for your child's rights. They ensure your child gets treated relatively everywhere – at work, school, you name it. They're the ones who step up and say, "Hey, this isn't fair," when something isn't right. They make sure that your child gets the same chances as everyone else.

But disability advocates have another superpower. They're good at dealing with paperwork and rules that need clarification. If you're feeling lost in a maze of forms and legal stuff, they're like the detectives who help solve the mystery. They ensure you complete everything right and that no one breaks the rules for your child's rights.

Finally, we have the medical professionals. These are the doctors, nurses, and therapists who help take care of your child's health. They're like a well-coordinated sports team, passing the ball back and forth to ensure your child gets the best care.

They also help when you make tough choices about your child's health. I clearly explained your options to help you make the best decision. They're like the coach who enables you to figure out the best plays for your team.

So even though caring for your grown-up child with disabilities can sometimes seem complicated, remember you're part of a team. Social workers, disability advocates, and medical professionals are on your side.

It's okay to ask for help when you need it. Every person is unique and requires special care. But with your strong team, you can ensure your child gets the best support possible. Remember, these professionals are here for you and your child. They're ready to help and cheer you every step of the way.

So let's get out there and make the most of this journey, team! Together, we can navigate through any challenge that comes our way.

Community Resources

When we think about local organizations, imagine them as your community superheroes, always ready to swoop in with help. These groups deeply understand the unique challenges your adult child with disabilities might face. The Arc, NAMI, and Autism Speak are your experts, providing knowledge, support, and advocacy. Their role goes beyond giving advice. They provide essential knowledge about your child's condition. But their support continues beyond there. These organizations promote your child's rights, ensuring they have the same opportunities.

Assistance for those with disabilities is provided by organizations such as UCP, Easter Seals, and NDSS. They tailor their programs and services to address your child's needs directly. But what about when it's time for your child to find work? That's where the Job Accommodation Network, or JAN, steps in. They aid with job-seeking and workplace adjustments.

Imagine a world rich with fun, stimulating, and accessible activities custom-made for your child. That's the beautiful world of social and recreational programs. The Special Olympics isn't just about games and competitions. It's about nurturing confidence, fostering camaraderie, and empowering participants. Meanwhile, Best Buddies International goes beyond friendship. It's a network where your child can develop valuable life skills, grow into leadership roles, and find meaningful employment.

And there are more! Organizations like the Miracle League, Art-Reach, and Disabled Sports USA open the doors to many exciting activities. From baseball to art to new sports activities, these groups offer spaces where your child can engage, learn, and thrive in a supportive environment. These programs improve social skills, physical health, and self-esteem.

Figure 21. Parents at a Community Center

But what about preparing your child for the world of work? That's where vocational support comes in. Goodwill Industries, The Arc, and Vocational Rehabilitation Agencies can be seen as career mentors. They provide job training and support, almost like school. They help your child learn essential job skills, and when ready, they offer guidance in finding suitable employment.

And there's more. JAN, Project SEARCH, and the Ability One Program take the extra step to ensure your child finds a job that fits them just right. Your child's rights are protected in the workplace, and they feel valued due to the diligent work of JAN, Project SEARCH, and the Ability One Program.

BUILDING A SUPPORT NETWORK

So, remember, on this journey, you're never alone. These organizations and programs are part of your extended family. They're ready to help your child learn, socialize, enjoy, and find meaningful work. So, reach out to them and discover the wide world of support waiting to help your child live their best, most fulfilling life!

CHAPTER VII

Preparing Your Adult Child for Transition

As parents, we want our children to grow into independent adults, leading fulfilled lives. The journey might seem more complex when your child has a disability, but the goal remains. This chapter will focus on how you, as a parent, can empower your adult child with disabilities to transition smoothly into adulthood. We'll discuss fostering independence, developing life skills, decision-making, and transitions. Remember, the journey may not always be easy, but it will be worth it.

Firstly, let's delve into the importance of encouraging independence in your adult child. A vital component of this is teaching them life skills. Life skills go beyond academic learning and involve capabilities necessary for everyday life. Take personal care and hygiene, for example. Show them how to bathe, brush their teeth, or comb their hair. Make it a fun and engaging activity so they look forward to doing it alone.

Next, cooking and meal planning skills can bring significant accomplishment. Start small, maybe with a simple sandwich or salad. You can gradually introduce more complex recipes once they feel confident with the basics. This instills a sense of independence and encourages healthy eating habits.

Another essential life skill is budgeting and money management. Begin by identifying coins and notes, then move on to spending and saving, and finally, teach them budgeting.

Fostering decision-making abilities is critical for your adult child with disabilities. It begins with teaching them to evaluate options and understand potential consequences. Use simple, relatable situations at first, such as choosing between two snacks or picking a TV show. Please encourage them to think about the pros and cons of each option.

PREPARING YOUR ADULT CHILD FOR TRANSITION

Problem-solving and critical thinking go hand-in-hand with decision-making. They need to learn how to handle unexpected situations and find solutions. It can achieve this through role-playing or encouraging them to come up with solutions to minor issues.

Encourage independence and decision-making, then develop a transition plan. This plan will serve as a roadmap, helping your child achieve their goals and objectives. The first step here is to identify these goals, which can be short-term, like learning a new skill, or long-term, such as getting a job or living independently. It's essential that these goals are Specific, Measurable, Achievable, Relevant, and Time-bound (SMART), which will make it easier to track progress.

Stay in regular contact with service providers and your support network. Keep everyone involved updated on the progress and any obstacles encountered. You can schedule meetings to discuss advancements and tweak the plan as needed.

Remember, as parents of an adult child with disabilities, your goal is to create an environment where your child can thrive independently. The journey may have ups and downs, but your love, patience, and commitment will pave the way for a successful transition. And while this chapter offers guidance, remember that every child is unique. You know your child best, which makes you their greatest ally in preparing for adulthood.

Encouraging Independence

Personal care and hygiene are not just about cleanliness. It's about instilling a sense of self-pride and confidence in one's appearance. So, while teaching your child about brushing teeth or bathing, talk to them about why it's essential. Explain how being clean and well-groomed makes them feel good and leaves a positive impression on others.

When you teach cooking and meal planning, bonding with your child is a beautiful opportunity. Make these sessions fun and engaging. You can use this time to talk about nutrition and the importance of authentic food. Discuss the benefits of fruits and vegetables, the role of protein in building muscles, and the energy we get from carbohydrates. Please help your child become more confident in the kitchen and show them how to plan meals and eat healthily.

Figure 22. A child learning to cook

Money management lessons can be more than just learning about coins and notes. Use this as a chance to talk about the value of money and the importance of being responsible for it. As they handle their allowance, they will also learn about making choices and dealing with the consequences. For instance, if they spend their entire allowance on a toy, they must wait until the next allowance to buy something else. These are valuable life lessons that can help shape their understanding of money management in the future.

In decision-making skills, reinforce the concept of cause and effect. This means helping them understand that every action or decision will have an outcome. By linking their findings to the outcomes, they can begin to see the effects of their choices and learn from them. Use everyday situations as learning opportunities. For instance, if they want to play a video game but have homework, guide them through decision-making. What happens if they play the game first? What happens if they do their homework first? Let them make the decision and experience the outcome.

It's okay to make mistakes while developing problem-solving and critical-thinking skills. Explain to your child that errors are a natural part of life and provide opportunities to learn and grow. Encourage them to think of different solutions and be encouraged if the first solution fails.

Teaching your child these skills is about much more than just helping them become independent. It's about guiding them toward self-confidence, responsibility, and resilience. It's about empowering them to lead fulfilling, self-reliant lives. And there's no greater joy than seeing your child grow and succeed in their unique way. With your love and guidance, they can truly reach their full potential.

Developing a Transition Plan

Let's delve into the second crucial part of our journey: creating a transition plan. Think of a transition plan as a roadmap to guide your adult child with disabilities toward their goals and objectives. Just like a roadmap, it doesn't only tell you the destination but also shows you the different routes you can take to get there. And, of course, it's a map that you and your child will draw together based on what they want and where they hope to go in life.

First, you must sit down with your child and identify their goals and objectives. What do they dream of achieving in the future? Maybe they aspire to get a job, learn a new skill, or perhaps they want to live independently. These dreams can be big or small, long-term or short-term, but they should be what your child genuinely desires.

While setting these goals, remember to make them SMART—Specific, Measurable, Achievable, Relevant, and Time-bound. A SMART goal isn't just saying, "I want to cook," but "I want to learn how to cook spaghetti Bolognese by the end of this month." This way, you have a clear goal (cooking spaghetti Bolognese), a way to measure progress (can they do it or not), it's achievable and relevant to their interests, and it has a deadline (end of the month). SMART goals help make the process more organized and give a clear sense of direction.

Once you set your goals, it's time to contact the various service providers and your support network. These could include teachers, therapists, counselors, or other professionals involved in your child's life. Let them know about the transition plan and how they can contribute. They can offer valuable insights and suggestions based on their expertise and experience with your child.

Regular progress updates and meetings are an essential part of this process. They keep everyone involved on the same page and provide opportunities to celebrate successes, address challenges, and make necessary adjustments to the plan. Remember, the transition plan isn't set in stone; it's a dynamic document that changes and evolves with your child's progress and needs.

Last, remember this journey you and your child are taking together. You'll cheer them on as they take each step towards their goals, lend a listening ear when they're feeling down, and celebrate each victory, big or small. Helping your child through this transition takes patience, persistence, and love for a positive outcome. And in the end, that's what every parent hopes for—the joy of seeing their child thrive and lead a fulfilling life.

So, with the roadmap in your hands and your child by your side, you're all set to embark on this journey. Remember, it's not about how quickly you reach the destination but the growth, learning, and bonding that happens along the way. And no matter what, always remember that you're not alone on this journey. A community of parents, educators, and professionals has walked this path before and is ready to lend a helping hand.

CHAPTER VIII

Encouraging Parents to Take Action

As parents, we often face challenges and decisions that will shape our children's future. When you're the parent of an adult child with disabilities, these challenges can seem even more daunting. However, there's no need to fear. This chapter will provide practical advice and guidance to help you succeed. Let's journey together on this road, which may not always be easy, but with courage, support, and the right resources, it can become much more manageable.

Many parents feel overwhelmed and procrastinate when planning for their adult child with disabilities. It's an understandable reaction. You might ask, "Where do I start?" and "How can I possibly plan for all possibilities?" It's okay to feel this way. The key is to break the process down into manageable steps. Researching support resources could be a good start. This advisor can provide valuable information, guidance, and emotional support.

Sometimes the fear of the unknown can paralyze us. You may not know what the future holds for your child, and this uncertainty can be stressful. But remember, you're not alone in this journey. Countless resources include books, online articles, and community programs. Connecting with other families in similar situations can provide comfort and practical advice. These families have walked the path before you and can help you navigate it.

It's natural to want to secure your child's future, but where do you begin? Start by setting realistic timelines. Decide what you want to achieve in the next month, six months, or a year, and work towards these goals. Remember to celebrate your progress and accomplishments, no matter how small they may seem. It will motivate you to keep going.

Take your time with the burden. Share the responsibility with family and friends willing and able to help. Seek professional guidance, too. These experts have the knowledge and experience to help you navigate the complexities of planning for your child's future.

The journey may seem challenging, but remember, you're not alone. Take the first step, reach out, connect, and take action. Your love and determination will make a difference in your child's life. And that is the best gift any parent can give their child. Remember, every step forward, no matter how small a step in the right direction is.

Overcoming Common Obstacles

Life throws us many challenges. And when you're the parent of an adult child with disabilities, those challenges might seem even more significant than life. You might think, "How will I deal with this?" or "Where do I start?" Well, don't worry. You're not alone; there are ways to tackle these challenges and make them more manageable.

One big challenge you might face right now is feeling overwhelmed. It's like standing at the bottom of a tall mountain and looking up, thinking, "How am I ever going to climb to the top?" But just like mountain climbing, preparing for your child's future starts with a single step. Climbing a mountain step by step is an example of how breaking the task into smaller pieces makes it more accessible.

It could start with something as simple as making a list of everything your child might need, like medical care, housing, or help with daily tasks. Then, you can take each item on the list and start researching, talking to professionals, and figuring out what to do next. There are experts out there who specialize in adult care for individuals with disabilities. They can guide you, share valuable information with you, and provide you with much-needed emotional support. Remember, it's okay to ask for help.

Another hurdle that might hold you back is fear. It's normal to fear the unknown. You may worry about what the future holds for your child, and that can feel like a big, scary question mark. But you know what? Knowledge is like a bright flashlight that can light up the darkness of the unknown. The more you know, the less there is to fear.

Where can you get that knowledge? Resources like books about disability rights and online articles about adult care options are available. Every bit of information you gather makes that unknown a little less intimidating.

But you know what else can help? Other parents. There are families out there who have walked the same path you're on right now. They've faced the same fears, overcome the same challenges, and they can share their experiences with you. There's comfort in knowing you're not alone, and these families can give you that comfort and practical advice that you can use.

Preparing for your adult child's future may seem complicated, but remember, every journey begins with a single step. Make progress in small steps, ask for help, research, and connect with other families to overcome challenges. It might be tricky sometimes, but you can do this with determination, courage, and the right resources. After all, you're not just any parent – you're a superhero to your child, and together, you can climb this mountain.

Success Stories

Others who have gone this path before can offer us encouragement and guidance. Let's look at how the Smiths and Johnsons handled planning for a disabled adult child. Their stories are pretty different, yet they offer important lessons.

Have you heard about the Smith family? Their story shines like a beacon of success, lighting the way for others. They have a daughter, Lily, who has special needs. They rolled up their sleeves when planning for Lily's future and jumped right in. They researched adult care for those with disabilities through books, the internet, and experts.

Their next step was collaborating with professionals to set up a special needs trust. Think of it like a financial safety net for Lily, ensuring she has the resources, even when her parents can't be there. This trust was a significant step in their journey, ensuring Lily's financial safety.

Next, they focused on finding a suitable group home for Lily. They wanted a place where she would be comfortable, cared for, and happy. After visiting numerous homes and asking countless questions, they finally found the perfect place for her. It was a group home filled with caring staff and friendly residents where Lily could thrive.

But the Smiths didn't stop there. They contacted their extended family and friends and involved them in Lily's support network. Lily's support from this network gave her a diverse and rich web of security.

Now, let's talk about the Johnson family. Their story, while different from the Smiths', offers important lessons. The Johnsons have a son, Max, and a daughter, Jane, and Max has unique needs. The Johnsons' journey was rockier, primarily because they needed to plan adequately for Max's future.

Max and Jane faced many challenges because of this lack of planning. Their difficulty highlighted the importance of knowing government benefits and legal options for adults with disabilities. They learned this the hard way, but their experience is a stark reminder for all of us about the necessity of thorough planning.

Despite these initial difficulties, the Johnsons learned something invaluable. They realized a support network's critical role in a child's transition to adult living. His family, friends, and advisors supported Max, making his transition smoother.

These two families' stories highlight the spectrum of experiences that can come from planning for an adult child with disabilities. The Smiths emphasize the importance of thorough research, collaboration with experts, financial security, locating a suitable place to live, and establishing a solid support system. Inadequate planning has consequences, as the Johnsons' story illustrates. But both families underline the vital role of a support network in ensuring a smooth transition for your child. These stories should encourage you and remind you that every family's journey is unique, but we can all learn and grow together.

Encouraging Parents to Take Action

You've made it this far and learned so much already! You're well-equipped to navigate the path ahead. But as we've learned from the Smith and Johnson families' stories, knowing is only part of the journey. The other part is taking action. Let's explore this together.

Every incredible journey begins with a single step; setting out on this journey with a good sense of direction is essential. That's where setting realistic timelines come in. Think of it as planning a road trip. Would you expect to travel from somewhere other than New York to California in a day? Similarly, planning for your adult child's future takes time and effort. It requires thought, time, and lots of baby steps.

First off, start by identifying short-term and long-term goals. Short-term goals could be tasks you can achieve in the next few weeks or months. For instance, your short-term goal could be researching potential group homes in your area or reading a book about disability rights. Long-term goals could include tasks that take time, like setting up a trust or finding employment for your child.

ENCOURAGING PARENTS TO TAKE ACTION

These goals will act like signposts on your road trip, guiding you. And remember, even if you're moving slowly, you're still making progress. Progress is not about speed but about direction. So, no matter how small your progress may seem, celebrate it! Found a potential group home? That's fantastic! Have you understood a complex legal document finally? That's wonderful! Each achievement is a cause for celebration.

However, as you embark on this journey, it's important to remember that you're not alone. You can – and should – share the responsibility with others. This is like your road trip buddies who can share driving duties or navigate while you focus on the road. Maybe you have a friend who's a talented researcher or a cousin who's a financial whiz. Don't hesitate to reach out and ask for their help. It does not mean this journey is to be taken alone; every bit of help lightens your load.

Also, just like taking your car to a mechanic before a road trip, it's vital to consult professionals during this journey. Social workers, financial advisors, and disability advocates can help you plan for your adult child's future. They can provide invaluable advice, answer your questions, and help lighten your load.

Taking action is easier than it might initially seem. It involves setting manageable goals, celebrating each accomplishment, and asking for help when needed. It's about moving forward, one step at a time, toward your destination. The journey may be challenging, but it comes with opportunities.

So, gear up, and let's embark on this journey together. You are not alone. You have your family, friends, professionals, and this guide to accompany you. Each step you take is a step closer to a secure future. You can do this, and I'm here, cheering you on every step of the way!

CHAPTER IX

Looking Ahead

Well, you are done! You've been working very hard on this journey. We are proud of you! You've created a robust plan for your remarkable child's future. Your love, dedication, and hard work truly shine. Let's look ahead and imagine what could come next.

When your child is young, it might feel like you're always busy planning. You've prepared a roadmap with everything they need to grow and succeed. You've helped your child find a community, become more independent, and learn new skills. But remember, the plan is not the end—it's just the beginning.

Now, let's picture the future. Maybe your child will work at a job they love, or maybe they'll go to college. Perhaps they'll enjoy hobbies or create beautiful art. It's going to be amazing watching them shine! Every day, your child is learning and growing, just like you. Their future is bright and full of possibilities.

But don't worry if there are bumps along the road. Life can be unpredictable. It's okay if things don't always go according to plan. Every challenge is a chance to learn and grow together. And remember, you're not alone. You have a team of people who care and are here to support you.

Looking ahead, it's essential to keep updating your plan. As your child grows and changes, the plan will too. Regularly check in, update goals, and celebrate victories, big or small. And always remember to take time for yourself, too, because your well-being matters.

This journey might be challenging, but it will undoubtedly be rewarding. As you look to the future, remember how far you've come. Your hard work, patience, and love have made an enormous difference. The future is bright, and your child is ready to shine!

Congratulations again on all you've achieved. You are doing a great job. Let's keep looking ahead together, supporting and celebrating your child every step of the way.

CHAPTER X

Appendices

A.   Glossary of Terms

This section could contain various terms pertinent to the care and understanding of a person with a disability. Here are some examples:

504 Plan: A plan developed to ensure that a child who has a disability identified under the law and is attending an elementary or secondary educational institution receives accommodations that will ensure their academic success and access to the learning environment.

Ableism: Discrimination and social prejudice against people with disabilities or perceived as having disabilities. Ableism characterizes persons as defined by their disabilities and inferior to the non-disabled.

Americans with Disabilities Act (ADA): A civil rights law that prohibits discrimination against individuals with disabilities in all areas of public life, including jobs, schools, transportation, and all public and private places open to the general public.

Assistive Technology: Any device, software, or equipment that helps people work around their challenges. This can range from wheelchairs and hearing aids to speech-to-text software and screen readers.

Behavioral Therapy: A term encompassing various techniques used to change maladaptive behaviors. The focus is on current behavior and how to change it.

Community Integration: The opportunity to live in the community and be valued for one's uniqueness and abilities, just like everyone else. Community integration encompasses housing, employment, education, leisure, recovery and wellness, and citizenship.

Conservatorship: A legal concept in the United States that allows a judge to grant a guardian or a protector the authority to manage the financial affairs and daily life of another person due to physical or mental limitations or old age.

Developmental Disability: A diverse group of chronic conditions due to mental or physical impairments that arise before adulthood. Developmental disabilities cause individuals living with them many difficulties in certain areas of life, especially in language, mobility, learning, self-help, and independent living.

Direct Support Professional (DSP): Professionals who assist individuals with physical disabilities and intellectual disabilities to lead self-directed lives and contribute to the community, assists with activities of daily living, and encourages attitudes and behaviors that enhance community inclusion.

Disability Advocate: A person who supports and stands up for the rights of individuals with disabilities. Advocates can be professionals, family members, or even individuals with disabilities.

Early Intervention: A system of services that helps babies and toddlers with developmental delays or disabilities. Early intervention focuses on helping eligible babies and toddlers learn the basic and brand-new skills that typically develop during the first three years of life.

Free and Appropriate Public Education (FAPE): An educational right of children with disabilities in the United States guaranteed by the Rehabilitation Act of 1973 and the Individuals with Disabilities Education Act (IDEA).

Group Home: A private residence for children or adults with chronic disabilities. These homes usually have six or fewer occupants and are staffed 24 hours daily by trained caregivers.

Guardianship: A legal process in which someone (usually a family member) is appointed to make decisions for another person (the ward) who cannot make decisions for themselves due to a physical or mental disability.

Home and Community-Based Services (HCBS): Services provided by Medicaid that allow individuals to receive care in their home or community rather than in institutional settings.

Inclusion: Inclusion in education refers to a model wherein students with special needs spend most or all their time with non-special needs students.

Individualized Education Program (IEP): A document developed for each public school child who needs special education. The IEP is created through a team effort and reviewed at least once a year.

Least Restrictive Environment (LRE): A principle that governs the education of students with disabilities and other special needs by placing them in the least restrictive environment appropriate to their needs.

Life Skills: Skills that an individual can learn to function independently in society. They can be abilities for adaptive and positive behavior that enable individuals to deal effectively with the demands and challenges of everyday life, such as self-care, managing money, using public transportation, or preparing meals.

Medicaid: A state and federal program that provides health coverage for some low-income people, families and children, pregnant women, the elderly, and people with disabilities.

Occupational Therapy: A type of therapy that helps individuals achieve independence in all facets of their lives. For children with developmental disabilities, it often involves play activities that make therapeutic tasks more fun and engaging.

Person-Centered Planning: A process designed to assist someone in planning their life and support them. It is used most often as a life planning model to enable individuals with disabilities or otherwise requiring support to increase their self-determination and improve their independence.

APPENDICES

Physical Therapy: A form of treatment that focuses on movement and function when someone is affected by injury, disease, or disability. Physical therapy can involve exercises, manual therapy, education, and advice.

Reasonable Accommodation: A modification or adjustment to a job, the work environment, or how things are usually done during the hiring process. These modifications enable an individual with a disability to have an equal opportunity to get a job, perform job duties, and enjoy the benefits and privileges of employment.

Respite Care: A service that provides short-term relief for primary caregivers. This can be arranged for just an afternoon or several days in a row. Respite care can be provided at home, healthcare facilities, or adult day centers.

Section 504: Part of the Rehabilitation Act of 1973 prohibits discrimination based on disability in programs receiving federal financial assistance, as well as in the federal sector and the U.S. Postal Service.

Self-Advocacy: When people with disabilities speak up for themselves. This means that although a person may receive support from others, the individual is entitled to control their own resources and how they are directed.

Special Needs Trust: A legal arrangement that holds assets for a person with a disability. The purpose of the trust is to supplement any benefits the person may receive from government programs. A properly drafted special needs trust will allow the beneficiary to receive government benefits while still receiving funds from the trust.

Supplemental Security Income (SSI): A United States government program that provides stipends to low-income people aged (65 or older), blind, or disabled.

Supported Employment: A method of working with disabled people and other disadvantaged populations to overcome barriers to getting and keeping a job. This can involve job coaches, transportation assistance, assistive technology, specialized training, and individualized job duties.

Universal Design: The design and composition of an environment so that it can be accessed, understood, and used to the greatest extent possible by all people, regardless of their age, size, ability, or disability.

Vocational Rehabilitation: A set of services offered to individuals with disabilities designed to enable participants to attain skills, resources, attitudes, and expectations needed to compete in the interview process, get a job, and keep a job.

B.　　List of Resources and Organizations

1. National and Local Disability Organizations

This includes contact information, the mission of the organizations, and their services.

The Arc: An organization that supports people with intellectual and developmental disabilities throughout their lifetimes. They offer resources on topics including education, employment, and health. Website: www.thearc.org

National Association of Councils on Developmental Disabilities (NACDD): NACDD is the national association for the 56 Councils on Developmental Disabilities (DD Councils) across the United States and territories. Website: www.nacdd.org

Autism Society of America: Offers resources for individuals with autism, family members, and professionals. Website: www.autism-society.org

2. Legal and Financial Resources

This would include contact information, areas of expertise, and services offered.

National Disability Rights Network (NDRN): The nonprofit membership organization for the federally mandated Protection and Advocacy (P&A) Systems and the Client Assistance Programs (CAP) for individuals with disabilities. Website: www.ndrn.org

Special Needs Alliance: A national organization comprising attorneys dedicated to the practice of disability and public benefits law. Website: www.specialneedsalliance.org

The ABLE National Resource Center (ANRC): Provides information about federal – and state-related benefits of ABLE accounts. These accounts allow people with disabilities and their families to save for future expenses. Website: www.ablenrc.org

3. Medical and Support Service Providers

This could include a list of recommended local therapists, physicians, and rehabilitation centers, along with contact information and areas of expertise.

American Occupational Therapy Association (AOTA): The AOTA can help locate an occupational therapist who works with adults with disabilities. Website: www.aota.org

National Adult Day Services Association (NADSA): NADSA provides a directory of adult day services nationwide. Website: www.nadsa.org

Aging and Disability Resource Centers (ADRCs): Nationwide, state-based centers designed to help older adults and people with disabilities and their caregivers identify and access services and support. Website: www.adrc-tae.acl.gov

4. Housing and Living Arrangement Resources

Department of Housing and Urban Development (HUD): HUD offers housing assistance and other programs for people with disabilities. Website: www.hud.gov

The Center for Universal Design in Housing: Provides resources and guidance on creating accessible and inclusive living environments. Website: www.universaldesign.org

The Corporation for Supportive Housing: This organization works to advance housing solutions that deliver three powerful outcomes: 1) improved lives for the most vulnerable people, 2) maximized public resources and 3) strong, healthy communities. Website: www.csh.org

5. Employment Resources

Job Accommodation Network (JAN): Offers guidance on workplace accommodations and disability employment issues. Website: www.askjan.org

Vocational Rehabilitation Services: A federal-state program that helps people with disabilities find and maintain employment. You can find local offices through the state government's website.

AbilityJobs: The leading career site for individuals with disabilities. Website: www.abilityjobs.com

6. Mental Health Resources

National Alliance on Mental Illness (NAMI): NAMI provides advocacy, education, support, and public awareness so all individuals and families affected by mental illness can build better lives. Website: www.nami.org

Mental Health America (MHA): MHA has an online tool to help locate local mental health services. Website: www.mhanational.org

Depression and Bipolar Support Alliance (DBSA): DBSA provides hope, help, support, and education to improve the lives of people with mood disorders. Website: www.dbsalliance.org

These are just a few examples of resources available. Remember, these resources can vary by location, and some may be more relevant to certain individuals depending on the specific nature of their disability. Always do additional research to find the most appropriate resources for your situation.

APPENDICES

C.   Sample Letter of Intent

This would be a detailed letter that parents or guardians write for their child with a disability, describing the child's history, daily routine, medical needs, likes and dislikes, etc. This is not a legal document but helps guide future caregivers, trustees, and others involved in the person's care.

A letter of intent is important for parents of children with disabilities. It will provide future caregivers and trustees with information about your child's needs, routines, and history. While it is not legally binding, it can offer significant guidance on providing for your child's well-being.

Here is a general template for a letter of intent:

[Your Name]

[Your Address]

[City, State, Zip]

[Date]

To whom it may concern,

I am writing this letter of intent to provide some guidance regarding the care of our child, [Child's Full Name], who has a disability. This letter is not a legally binding but is meant to communicate our wishes for [Child's First Name]'s future care and life experiences.

I. Family History

[In this section, provide a brief overview of your family history, including your family members' names, significant dates (like marriages, divorces, or deaths), and any other information you feel is essential for your child's caregiver to know.]

APPENDICES

II. Description of Disability

[Provide a detailed description of your child's disability. Explain how it affects their daily life, their level of independence, and their need for assistance.]

III. Daily Routine

[Describe your child's typical daily routine, including any activities or hobbies they enjoy. Mention their meal preferences, bedtime, medications, or other daily tasks.]

IV. Medical Care

[List your child's current medical providers, their contact information, and why they currently see each one. Explain any regular treatments or medications they need.]

V. Educational and Vocational History

[Provide information about your child's educational background, including any schools they've attended or programs they've been a part of. If applicable, detail their vocational history and future job prospects or aspirations.]

VI. Social Relationships

[Describe your child's social connections, including friends, close relatives, and community or social groups they are a part of. Explain any crucial dynamics or ongoing social engagements.]

VII. Behavioral Management

[If applicable, discuss any behavioral management techniques that work for your child, including rewards, routines, or disciplines. This section may also include any known triggers or stressors.]

APPENDICES

VIII. Personal Preferences

[Describe your child's likes and dislikes, including favorite foods, activities, music, and any other preferences that might be useful for a caregiver to know.]

IX. Future Hopes and Wishes

[Finally, write about your aspirations for your child's future, including living situation, social activities, employment, and more.]

This letter is meant to comprehensively understand [Child's First Name]'s needs and desires. We trust that it will be a helpful guide for future caregivers.

Thank you for your attention to these matters.

Sincerely,

[Your Name]

Remember, this is a template and should be customized to fit your child's specific situation. Your letter of intent should be updated periodically to reflect changes in your child's life and needs.

D.   Sample Special Needs Trust Document

This is a detailed, legally accurate document that outlines the terms of the trust, including the designation of the trustee, the purpose of the trust, and specific instructions for the trustee in managing and disbursing the trust assets.

Drafting a trust document requires careful planning and professional expertise in estate planning and law, particularly concerning individuals with disabilities. Therefore, it's strongly recommended to consult with a qualified attorney to ensure all legal requirements are met, and your child's interests are adequately protected.

That being said, below is a very simplified example of what a special needs trust document could look like:

THIS SPECIAL NEEDS TRUST AGREEMENT, made this [Day] day of [Month, Year], by and between [Your Full Name], residing at [Your Full Address], from now on referred to as the "Settlor," and [Trustee's Full Name], residing at [Trustee's Full Address], from now on referred to as the "Trustee."

1. Declaration of Trust: Settlor does at this moment deliver, and the Trustee accepts the property described in Schedule A attached hereto and agrees to hold the same IN TRUST, upon the terms and conditions from now on set forth, for the benefit of [Beneficiary's Full Name], a disabled individual residing at [Beneficiary's Full Address], from now on referred to as the "Beneficiary."

2. Terms of Trust: The principal of this Trust and any undistributed income shall be held, managed, and distributed for the use and benefit of the Beneficiary by the terms and conditions outlined in this Agreement.

3. Use of Trust Property: The Trustee is authorized to expend such amounts of income and principal of the Trust as the Trustee, in their sole discretion, deems necessary or appropriate for the support, education, care, comfort, and welfare of the Beneficiary.

4. Trustee Powers: The Trustee shall have the power to invest and reinvest the trust property, to sell or lease property, to make repairs or improvements, or to hold any portion of the trust property unproductive for such period as the Trustee may deem advisable.

5. Trust Termination: Upon the death of the Beneficiary, the remaining trust property shall be distributed as specified in the document.

IN WITNESS of which, the Settlor has signed and sealed this

APPENDICES

Agreement, and the Trustee has hereunto set their hand and seal,
as of the day and year first above written.

[Your Full Name] [Trustee's Full Name]

Settlor Trustee

Remember, this is a highly simplified sample of a special needs trust document and only includes a few terms and conditions that your trust should include. Always consult with a legal professional when creating a special needs trust.

E.   Sample Family Caregiver Agreement

A sample of this agreement would lay out terms, such as the type of care to be provided, the amount of time expected for caregiving, the compensation (if any) for the caregiver, and any other responsibilities or expectations.

A Family Caregiver Agreement is a contract that documents the understanding between a caregiver (often a family member) and the person receiving care. It specifies the type of care that will be provided, the amount of compensation (if any), and other terms. Creating an agreement helps avoid misunderstandings and is necessary for Medicaid considerations. Please consult a legal professional to ensure this document meets your family's needs and complies with local laws.

FAMILY CAREGIVER AGREEMENT

This agreement is entered into on this [Day] day of [Month,
Year], between [Caregiver's Full Name], henceforth known as
"Caregiver," and [Recipient's Full Name], henceforth known as
"Recipient," both of whom are signing voluntarily.

1. Services: The Caregiver will provide the following services to
the Recipient:

[In this section, outline all the services the caregiver will
provide. For example, Assistance with daily living activities,

medication management, meal preparation, transportation to appointments, etc.]

2. Schedule: The services will be provided according to the following schedule:

[Specify when the caregiver will be working. For example, from 9 AM to 5 PM Monday to Friday.]

3. Compensation: The Caregiver will be compensated as follows:

[Indicate whether the caregiver will be paid, and if so, how much and how often. For example, The Caregiver will be compensated at $X per hour, to be paid monthly. If the caregiver is not being paid, state this explicitly.]

4. Termination: This Agreement may be terminated by either party with [Number of Days] days' notice or immediately in the case of a severe breach of this Agreement.

5. Other Terms:

[Include any other terms or conditions relevant to your situation. For example, how costs like transportation will be reimbursed, or what happens if the caregiver needs to take a day off.]

We, the undersigned, agree to the terms and conditions outlined above.

[Caregiver's Full Name] [Recipient's Full Name]

Date: _____ Date: _____

Please remember that this is a simplified example and may include only some necessary details for your situation. It is recommended to seek legal advice to ensure the agreement is comprehensive and legally sound.

APPENDICES

F.   Checklist for Choosing Housing Options

This checklist would include considerations like whether the housing is fully accessible, if necessary, whether support services are nearby, cost and affordability, the area's safety, and whether the housing offers an integrated community setting.

Selecting an appropriate housing option for an adult child with disabilities can be challenging. Several factors must be considered, from the level of care and support required to their independence and personal preferences. Here is an essential checklist to guide you through this process:

1. Level of Care Needed

☐ Does the housing option provide adequate care for my child's needs (physical, mental, and emotional)?
☐ Are medical services readily available if needed?
☐ Is there enough staff to handle the residents' needs?
☐ Are the staff appropriately trained to handle my child's specific disability?

2. Living Environment

☐ Is the living space clean, safe, and well-maintained?
☐ Are there provisions for residents with physical disabilities (ramps, handrails, etc.)?
☐ Is the living environment comfortable and conducive to my child's well-being?
☐ Does living space offer privacy?

3. Social Environment

☐ Are there opportunities for social interaction and recreational activities?
☐ Does the housing option encourage community participation?
☐ Are there mechanisms in place to handle disputes between residents?

4. Independence and Personal Preference

- ☐ Does this housing option align with my child's preferences?
- ☐ Does it encourage independence to the level my child is comfortable with and capable of?

5. Location

- ☐ Is the location convenient for visits from family and friends?
- ☐ Is it near necessary amenities like hospitals, shopping centers, and public transportation?

6. Cost and Financing

- ☐ Can we afford the cost of this housing option?
- ☐ Does the housing option accept payments through governmental programs, insurance, etc.?
- ☐ Are there any hidden costs we need to be aware of?

7. Future Needs

- ☐ Can this housing option accommodate changes in my child's health or disability status?
- ☐ How easy is it to transition to a different level of care if needed in the future?

Remember, this essential checklist should be personalized based on your child's specific needs and preferences. Always do thorough research and consider seeking advice from professionals or others who have faced similar decisions.

APPENDICES

G.   Transition Planning Worksheet

This would be a guide or workbook to plan the transition from school to work or adult life. It could include steps for identifying the individual's interests and skills, potential employment or career options, necessary education or training, and support to help them achieve their goals. This document might be created with input from teachers, counselors,

Transition planning is the process of preparing students with disabilities for life after high school. It includes academic preparation, job training, and life skills development. Here's a sample transition planning worksheet:

Student's Name:
Date of Birth:
School:
Expected Graduation Date:

1. Current Level of Functioning
Academic Performance:
Social Skills:
Independent Living Skills:
Employment/Vocational Skills:
Health/Medical Status:

2. Post-School Goals

Educational/Vocational Training Goals:
Employment Goals:
Independent Living Goals:

3. Transition Services Needed

Course of Study:
Career/Vocational Education:
Independent Living Skills Training:
Community Experiences:
Functional Vocational Assessment:

4. Annual Goals that Support Transition

Academic Goals:
Social/Behavioral Goals:
Vocational Goals:
Independent Living Goals:

5. Agency Involvement

Agencies to be Involved in Transition:
Services Provided by These Agencies:
Contact Information for These Agencies:

6. Follow-Up

Progress Towards Goals:
Adjustments to Plan (if needed):

This worksheet is a simplified template. Transition planning usually involves a team of people, including the student, parents, teachers, and other professionals. It's essential to revise the plan periodically and make changes based on the student's progress and changing needs.

CHAPTER XI

Acknowledgments

Writing this book, "A Comprehensive Guide to Planning for Your Adult Child with Disabilities," has been a profound journey of understanding, empathy, and learning. This journey would have been more challenging without many generous and understanding individuals' help, support, and guidance. I am taking a moment in this chapter to acknowledge and extend my heartfelt gratitude to all of them.

I want to express my deepest gratitude to Dr. Harlan Kilstein, who helped me start this endeavor.

I sincerely thank the numerous experts and professionals in disability care and advocacy. Their research, experiences, and perspectives have been instrumental in making this guide comprehensive and relevant. The content from the work of Dr. James D. Thompson, Dr. Maria Peterson, and Dr. Eleanor Forbes was beneficial.

I am particularly grateful to the teams and members of the non-profit organizations, 'Pathways for Independence' and 'Unified Care Providers,' who work tirelessly to improve the lives of individuals with disabilities. Their resources have significantly enriched the content of this book.

My most profound appreciation to my family for their love, patience, and understanding. Their endless support has been a beacon during the most challenging times. I am incredibly grateful to my spouse, whose unwavering belief in the importance of this work propelled me forward when times were tough.

Lastly, I want to acknowledge the wonderful community of individuals with disabilities and their families worldwide. You have taught me resilience, strength, and the enduring power of love. You have shown that while challenges can be significant, the human spirit is more excellent.

Every word in this book is a testament to the collective effort of all these incredible individuals. Thank you all. May this guide be the companion you need on your journey, easing your path and shedding light on your way forward.

With the deepest gratitude,
Dayanand Shahapurkar

Author Bio

Dayanand is a Metallurgical Engineer, which means he knows about working with metals. He studied and earned a Ph.D. in Metallurgy from Penn State University. After working for 35 years in places where things are made, he retired in 2016.

In 2008, his wife got sick with a neurological disorder that made her disabled. Since then, Dayanand, his son Rajiv, and his daughter Priya have been caring for her. This experience made him feel for other families who also take care of their loved ones with disabilities. He understands how challenging and vital this job is.

In March 2023, Dayanand met Harlan Kilstein, an entrepreneur and technology expert. They talked about info products, which teach others helpful information. They both realized a need for a book to help families care for their loved ones with disabilities.

Dayanand wrote this book with the hope of helping parents, caregivers, and children with disabilities. He wants to show understanding, kindness and make the world a more inclusive place for everyone.

Made in the USA
Middletown, DE
08 November 2023

42168679R00053